Title Page

Through Darkness to Destiny

An Inmate's Journey to Redemption and Purpose, with Guide to Life After Prison and Practical Steps for Reintegration and Success

by

Jamal Carter

Copyright Page

© 2024 by **Jamal Carter**

All rights reserved. No part of this book may be reproduced, stored in a retrieval system, or transmitted in any form or by any means, electronic, mechanical, photocopying, recording, or otherwise, without the prior written permission of the publisher, except for the use of brief quotations in a book review.

Preface

When I first sat down to write this book, I wasn't sure how to begin. How do you take a life marked by pain, poor choices, and imprisonment, and turn it into a story of hope and redemption? For many years, I didn't believe such a transformation was even possible. I thought the mistakes I had made would forever define me. I believed I was destined to live in the shadows of my past.

But prison has a way of forcing you to confront the truth—about yourself, your decisions, and your life. It strips away the excuses, the distractions, and the false narratives you've built up. It leaves you face-to-face with the person you've become. And, in my case, it left me asking the question I had been avoiding for years: "Is this it? Is this all my life will amount to?"

For a long time, I was convinced the answer was yes. I had fallen too far, caused too much damage, and burned too many bridges to ever find my way back. But life, as I've come to realize, has a way of offering second chances, even when you don't think you deserve them. And sometimes, those second chances come in the most unexpected ways.

This book is about my journey through those second chances. It's not just about my time behind bars—it's about what I learned in that dark place and how it changed me forever. It's about finding hope when it seemed like none existed and discovering a purpose that gave my life meaning.

More importantly, this book is for anyone who feels lost, stuck, or defined by their mistakes. It's for those still walking through the darkness, whether in a literal prison cell or the prison of their circumstances. I want this story to show that it's never too late to change, to grow, and to find redemption. Your past doesn't have to define your future.

So, whether you're an inmate, a family member, or simply someone looking for hope in the face of adversity, I hope my story offers you the encouragement you need to keep moving forward.

I didn't write this book because I have all the answers—I wrote it because I've been where you are, and I found a way out. Now, I want to help you find yours.

— Jamal Carter

Gratitude

As I sit here, reflecting on the journey that brought me to this point, I am overwhelmed by the many people who have played a role in my story—people who believed in me when I didn't believe in myself, and those who stood by me through the darkest times. This book would not exist without their unwavering support, encouragement, and guidance.

First and foremost, I want to thank God for the grace and mercy that carried me through. There were moments when I was ready to give up, but I found strength in knowing that His plan for me was bigger than the mistakes I had made. For that, I am forever grateful.

To my family, especially my mother, who never stopped praying for me, even when I gave her every reason to. Your love and faith in me kept me grounded, and I will always be thankful for the sacrifices you made to help me find my way back.

To my friends who stood by me through thick and thin, especially those who visited, wrote letters, and reminded me that I still had a life worth living. Your loyalty and support kept me going when the days were long, and hope seemed distant.

I am deeply grateful to the mentors and counselors I met while incarcerated. You showed me that even in the darkest places, there is room for growth, change, and redemption. You taught me to believe in myself again, and that belief has fueled this journey of transformation.

To the inmates who walked this path with me, I see you. You are a part of this story too. Your strength, courage, and resilience inspired me every day. We found hope together, and I am forever thankful for the brotherhood we built within those walls.

A heartfelt thanks to my editor and the publishing team for helping bring this story to life. Your dedication and hard work ensured that these words could reach those who need them most, and for that, I am truly appreciative.

Lastly, to my readers—thank you for taking the time to walk with me through this journey. Whether you're reading this as an inmate, a family member, or someone looking for hope, I am honored that you've allowed me to share my story with you. I hope these pages inspire you to keep pushing forward, no matter where you are in life.

This book is not just mine—it belongs to everyone who has played a role in my life. I could not have done this alone, and for that, I am endlessly grateful.

— Jamal Carter

TABLE OF CONTENTS

Preface

Gratitude

Prologue

The Crossroads

Chapter 1

The Fall

Chapter 2

The Darkness Within

Chapter 3

The Prison Code

Chapter 4

A Glimmer of Hope

Chapter 5

Finding Purpose Behind Bars

Chapter 6

Redemption in the Smallest Acts

Chapter 7

Facing the Outside World

Chapter 8

Walking the Path of Purpose

Chapter 9

A New Chapter

Chapter 10

Guide to Life After Prison: Practical Steps for Reintegration and Success

Epilogue

Letters to My Younger Self

Prologue

The Crossroads

They say life gives you choices, but looking back, it didn't always feel like I had any. My name is Jamal Carter, and if you're reading this, you're about to hear the story of how a man can go from having nothing but a life of chaos and pain to finding purpose in the most unlikely of places—behind bars.

It wasn't always clear to me when my life went off track. Growing up on the South Side, it was all about survival. The streets didn't care who you were, and the only thing that mattered was making it through each day without getting caught up. But somewhere along the line, I hit a point where I wasn't just trying to survive—I was making choices that would land me in a place I thought I'd never see: prison.

I remember the night like it was yesterday. The sky was darker than usual, the air heavy and there was a tension that sat on my shoulders like a weight I couldn't shake. It wasn't my first time running with the wrong crowd, but this time something felt different. I was 23, reckless, and thinking I had the world figured out. That night, everything changed.

We were out late, doing what we always did—looking for fast money, trouble, or both. It started as a small job, something I thought would go unnoticed, but the cops were quicker than we expected. Within minutes, sirens echoed through the streets, and my heart raced as we scattered in different directions. I thought I could outrun them—I'd done it before—but that night, the streets betrayed me. The next thing I knew, I was cuffed, shoved into the back of a squad car, and staring at a future that felt as dark as the sky above.

Prison wasn't something I ever saw for myself, but life has a funny way of throwing you into the fire when you least expect it. The trial came and went in a blur. My public defender barely knew my name, and before I knew it, I was standing in front of a judge who didn't care where I came from or what led me down this path. All he saw was another young Black man who'd made the wrong choice.

And just like that, my freedom was gone.

As they led me out of the courtroom, I remember thinking: *This is it. This is my life now.* I wasn't thinking about redemption or second chances. All I could feel was anger and regret, mixed with a deep sense of shame. My momma was in the back of the courtroom, tears streaming down her face. She raised me better than this, and yet there I was, another statistic in a broken system.

But here's the thing—I didn't write this book to tell you how the system failed me, or to give you excuses for the choices I made. I'm here to tell you how, in the depths of that darkness, I found a light. I found a way to turn everything around and make something out of the mess I had made.

Prison didn't break me, but it sure as hell tested me. It wasn't easy, and I made plenty of mistakes along the way, but through it all, I learned that redemption isn't about what the world sees. It's about what you see when you look in the mirror.

This is my story—a story of falling, of being knocked down, and of finding the strength to get back up. If you're an inmate reading this, know that I've been where you are. I've walked those same hallways, felt that same despair, and wondered if there was a way out.

There is.

It doesn't come easy, and it doesn't come overnight. But if you're willing to dig deep, if you're willing to face the parts of yourself you've been running from, there's a way out of the darkness. There's a way to turn your life around, no matter how far you've fallen.

So let's take this journey together. Through the pain, through the struggle, and eventually, to a place where you can find purpose. My name is Jamal Carter, and this is how I went from a prisoner to a man living with purpose.

Chapter 1

The Fall

I was born into a world that had its own rules, its codes of survival. The South Side of Chicago was all I knew—a place where hope felt more like a distant dream than a reality. Growing up, I didn't have much. My momma worked two jobs just to keep food on the table, and my dad, well, he wasn't in the picture. He left when I was just a baby, and the streets became the closest thing I had to a father figure. They taught me everything I thought I needed to know about how to survive.

By the time I was 10, I'd seen more than most grown men should. Drugs, violence, hunger—they were everyday things where I came from. My momma tried her best to keep me on the straight path, but it's hard to stay clean when everyone around you is living dirty. I used to watch her come home late from her job at the diner, her face tired and her hands aching from all the scrubbing and wiping she had to do. She'd collapse on the couch, barely able to speak, but every night she'd say the same thing before she fell asleep: "Jamal, baby, you gotta be better than this. You gotta rise above it."

I tried to listen. I tried to be the son she wanted me to be, but the streets had a pull on me that was stronger than anything she could say. It wasn't that I didn't want to rise above. It was just that, from where I stood, there didn't seem to be anything to rise to. All I saw was the hustle. The older guys on the block who had nice cars and flashy clothes—they weren't working two jobs at no diner. They were making money fast, living life big, and to a kid like me, that looked like the only way out.

I started running with the wrong crowd when I was about 12. At first, it was just small stuff—hanging around the corner, looking for the older boys when they were making deals. I'd get a few dollars here and there, enough to buy some new sneakers or help my momma with the bills when she didn't have enough. But the deeper I got into that life, the harder it was to pull away.

By the time I hit high school, I was fully caught up. The school didn't matter to me anymore. I barely showed up to class, and when I did, my mind wasn't on books or lessons. It was on the streets. The guys I ran with became my family, my brothers. We watched each other's backs, protected our turf, and made sure no one messed with us. We weren't a gang, at least not in the beginning. We were just trying to survive.

But survival came with a price. The more we pushed into the street life, the more we got noticed by the real gangs—the ones who ran the South Side. They didn't like new faces trying to make moves on their territory, and it wasn't long before things started to get serious. We had to prove ourselves if we wanted to stay in the game. That's when things started to spiral.

I remember the first time I held a gun. I was 16, and one of the older guys in the crew handed it to me after we had a run-in with a rival crew. "You need to protect yourself out here, Jamal," he said. His voice was calm like he was talking about something as simple as tying your shoes. But holding that cold steel in my hand felt like crossing a line I couldn't uncross. That gun was power, but it was also a weight—a weight that pulled me deeper into a life I wasn't sure I wanted.

At first, I only carried it for protection. The South Side wasn't a place you walked around without something to defend yourself. But carrying a gun changes you. It makes you feel like you can handle anything, like no one can touch you. And with that feeling came a recklessness I hadn't felt before.

It was around that time that I started getting into bigger trouble. Small-time hustling turned into bigger jobs—breaking into cars, running packages for the dealers, and eventually getting involved in armed robberies. Each time, I told myself it was just one more job, one more score to get me out of the hole I was in. But the hole kept getting deeper, and soon enough, I couldn't see a way out.

Then came the night that changed everything.

I had just turned 23, and by then, I was deep in the game. Me and my crew were doing bigger jobs, and the money was coming in faster. But with the money came the heat. The cops were starting to pay attention, and rival crews were gunning for us harder than ever. We were running out of moves, and everyone knew it. But instead of backing down, we decided to go bigger. We figured if we could pull off one big job, we could lay low for a while, maybe even get out of the game for good.

Looking back, I realize how foolish that thinking was. There's no "getting out" once you're in this deep. But at the time, we were desperate, and desperation makes you blind to the risks. We planned the job for weeks—a robbery at a local convenience store we knew was a front for some drug money. It was supposed to be quick and clean. In and out before anyone knew what happened.

But nothing ever goes as planned.

On the night of the job, things went wrong from the start. One of the guys got spooked, and before we knew it, the whole thing was a mess. Shots were fired, people were screaming, and we were scrambling to get out of there. I remember running through the streets, my heart pounding, trying to find a way out. The sirens were getting closer, and I knew it was only a matter of time before they caught up to us.

I thought I could outrun them. I thought I could disappear into the shadows like I had so many times before. But this time, there was nowhere to hide. The cops were on us quicker than I expected, and before I knew it, I was on the ground, face down, with handcuffs digging into my wrists.

That night was the beginning of the end. The next few months were a blur—court dates, lawyers, and a judge who looked at me like I was just another lost cause. My momma came to every hearing, her face filled with disappointment and pain. I'll never forget the look in her eyes the day they sentenced me. It was like a part of her died that day.

I was sentenced to 15 years. Fifteen years in a maximum-security prison for a robbery gone wrong. It felt like my life was over before it had even begun.

I can still hear the judge's words echoing in my mind: *"Fifteen years."* The courtroom was silent after that, the kind of silence that rings in your ears, heavy and suffocating. I didn't even react at first. It was like I was outside of myself, watching the whole thing happen from some distant place. Everything I'd done, all the choices I'd made, had led me to this exact moment.

But what hurt the most wasn't the sentence. It wasn't even the fact that I was going to prison. What hurt was looking up and seeing my momma sitting in the back row, her hands covering her face, her shoulders shaking as she cried. My heart broke right there. I had let her down in the worst way possible, and there was nothing I could do to take it back.

She raised me better than this. She always tried to keep me out of trouble, and always told me I could be more than what the streets had to offer. But I didn't listen. I thought I knew better. Now, I was going to spend the next 15 years paying for my mistakes, and she was going to have to live with that burden, too.

After the sentencing, they took me straight to a holding cell. The cold, hard bench beneath me was a cruel introduction to what was coming next. I sat there for hours, staring at the concrete walls, trying to make sense of what had just happened. My whole life was about to change, and I didn't know if I was strong enough to handle it.

The weeks leading up to my transfer to prison were some of the longest of my life. I spent most of that time in a county jail, surrounded by other men who were either awaiting trial or had just been sentenced like me. The place was tense, full of anger and fear. Fights broke out almost every day, and it didn't take long for me to realize that if I was going to survive, I had to stay sharp and keep my head down.

But staying out of trouble was easier said than done. The first time I got into a fight, it wasn't even my fault. One of the other inmates thought I was disrespecting him because I didn't make eye contact when he walked past me. That's all it took. In here, respect was everything, and the smallest sign of weakness could turn you into a target. So, when he stepped on me, I had no choice but to defend myself. The fight was over in minutes, but by the end of it, my knuckles were bloody, and I had a split lip. That was just the beginning.

By the time I was finally transferred to the state prison, I felt like I had already aged ten years. The day they put me on that bus, shackled at the wrists and ankles, I realized just how real this was about to get. This wasn't county jail anymore. This was the big leagues—maximum security. I had heard the stories about what happened to guys like me in prison. The violence, the gangs, the constant threat of danger. And I'd be lying if I said I wasn't scared.

The bus ride felt like a lifetime. Every mile we traveled took me farther away from the life I had known, and closer to a world I wasn't ready for. As I stared out the window, I couldn't help but think about how I had gotten here.

Every decision, every wrong turn, every moment where I could have done something different but didn't. It all added up to this.

When we finally arrived at the prison, the first thing I noticed was the barbed wire. It stretched as far as the eye could see, coiled on top of the tall concrete walls like a snake ready to strike. The place looked like a fortress, designed to keep us in and the rest of the world out. The bus stopped in front of a massive metal gate, and as it slowly opened, I felt my stomach tighten. This was it. My new home for the next 15 years.

They processed us like cattle, one by one. We were stripped down, searched, and given our prison uniforms—drab, gray jumpsuits that made us all look the same. I'll never forget the sound of the door slamming shut behind me when they locked me in my cell for the first time. That sound echoed in my head, and at that moment, it hit me: I was no longer free. My life, as I had known it, was over.

I spent the first few nights in that cell-wide awake, staring at the ceiling, wondering how I was going to survive this. The reality of my situation started to sink in, and with it came the weight of my choices. The anger I had carried for so long, the resentment, the feeling that the world owed me something—it all began to crumble under the pressure of where I was. There was no one to blame but myself.

But even as I sat there, feeling like I was at the lowest point in my life, I couldn't help but think about the people I had left behind. My momma, my little sister, the friends I had grown up with.

I had let them all down. I had become exactly what the world expected me to become—a statistic. Another young Black man caught up in the system.

That realization was hard to swallow. For so long, I had convinced myself that I was just doing what I had to do to survive. That the streets were my only option. But now, sitting in that cell, I couldn't escape the truth. I had made choices—choices that had consequences. And now, I was paying for them.

Prison life was exactly what I expected it to be, and at the same time, nothing like I could have imagined. On the surface, it was all about survival. You had to watch your back at all times, stay out of the wrong people's way, and never let your guard down. There were rules, and unspoken codes that everyone followed. If you didn't, you were in for a world of hurt.

But beneath all that, prison was something else. It was a place where time seemed to stand still, where the outside world faded away, and all you had was your thoughts to keep you company. And let me tell you, when you're stuck in a cell for 23 hours a day, those thoughts can be your worst enemy.

I spent a lot of time thinking about my past—about the choices I had made and the people I had hurt. At first, it was hard to face it. The guilt, the shame, it all felt like too much to bear. But the more I thought about it, the more I realized that I couldn't run from it anymore. I had to face it. I had to own up to the man I had become.

There were days when the anger would come back, burning inside me like a fire I couldn't put out. I would think about the system, about how it seemed designed to trap people like me, and I'd feel that familiar rage bubbling up again. But no matter how much I wanted to blame the world, deep down, I knew that I was the one who had put myself here.

The worst part about prison wasn't the violence or the isolation. It was the feeling of being forgotten. The world moved on without you. Life kept going for everyone on the outside, but for you, time just stopped. People stopped writing and stopped visiting. Even my momma, who had always been there for me, started coming around less and less. I couldn't blame her. I had caused her enough pain, and I knew that seeing me like this only made it worse.

But even as the world moved on without me, something inside me refused to give up. There was still a part of me, buried deep beneath the anger and regret, that believed I could be something more. That believed I could find a way out of this darkness.

Chapter 2

The Darkness Within

Prison does something to a man. It strips away everything you thought you knew about yourself and forces you to face the raw, unfiltered truth. The walls close in on you, and the silence becomes deafening. There's no escape from your mind, no distractions to take away the sting of your regrets. For the first few months, I tried to fight it. I tried to keep up the same front I had worn on the outside, but deep down, I was unraveling.

When I first walked through those prison gates, I told myself I could handle it. I had been through tough times before. Growing up on the South Side, I thought I had seen it all. But nothing could've prepared me for the kind of darkness that comes with being locked up. It's not just the physical bars or the guards watching your every move. It's the way prison gets into your head, the way it breaks you down piece by piece until there's almost nothing left.

At first, I was angry—angry at the world, angry at myself. I spent every day stewing in that anger, letting it consume me. I told myself that I was a victim, that the system had set me up to fail from the beginning. And in a lot of ways, I wasn't wrong. Growing up Black and poor in a neighborhood like mine, the odds were stacked against me from the start. But even as I tried to convince myself that it wasn't my fault, there was a voice in the back of my mind that I couldn't ignore.

You did this. You made those choices. Now you have to live with them.

I didn't want to hear that voice. It was easier to blame the streets, to blame my circumstances, than to take responsibility for the path I had chosen. But as the weeks turned into months, and the months into years, that voice got louder. No matter how much I tried to drown it out, it was always there, reminding me of the man I had become.

The hardest part of the prison wasn't the violence or the isolation. It was the weight of my guilt. Guilt for what I had done, for the people I had hurt, for the family I had abandoned. I couldn't stop thinking about my momma, how she had worked so hard to keep me out of trouble, how she had sacrificed so much for me, only for me to throw it all away. Every time I closed my eyes, I saw her face, the disappointment in her eyes the day I was sentenced. That image haunted me.

I tried to write to her at first, but the words never came out right. What could I say that would make it better? Sorry wasn't enough. Nothing I could say would undo the pain I had caused her. So, eventually, I stopped writing. I stopped calling. It was easier to disappear, to let the world forget about me than to face the hurt I had caused.

But prison doesn't let you hide. It forces you to confront the darkest parts of yourself, whether you want to or not. And for a long time, I wasn't ready to face that. I tried to keep up the tough-guy act, tried to pretend like I didn't care.

But the truth was, I was scared—scared of what would happen if I let go of the anger, scared of what I'd find if I looked too deep inside myself.

The other inmates could see it, too. Prison has a way of exposing your weaknesses, and if you're not careful, those weaknesses can be used against you. I kept my head down and tried to avoid trouble, but trouble has a way of finding you in a place like this. Fights broke out over the smallest things—a sideways glance, a bump in the cafeteria line, someone sitting in the wrong seat. Respect was everything, and if you didn't fight to keep yours, you'd lose it.

I remember one fight in particular. It was over something stupid—some guy thought I had disrespected him by cutting in line for the phones. I didn't even realize I had done it, but here, it didn't matter. Perception is reality, and if he thought I was trying to punk him, that was enough to start something. Before I knew it, fists were flying, and I was on the ground, my face pressed against the cold concrete, his fists pounding into me.

At that moment, as I lay there, bleeding and dazed, something inside me snapped. I had been holding onto so much anger, so much rage, and all of it came flooding out. I fought back with everything I had, not just against him, but against all the pain and frustration I had been carrying for so long. By the time the guards pulled us apart, I was a mess—bruised, and bleeding, but somehow feeling lighter, like I had let go of something that had been weighing me down.

After that, things changed. Not on the outside—prison was still a prison, and I was still just another inmate trying to survive—but on the inside, I started to see things differently. That fight forced me to confront the anger I had been holding onto for so long, and in doing so, I realized that it was destroying me.

The anger wasn't helping me survive. It was killing me.

For so long, I had blamed the world for my problems. I had convinced myself that I was just a product of my environment and that I had no choice but to live the life I had lived. But sitting in that cell, bruised and beaten, I started to see things differently. I started to see that the choices I had made—the decisions that had led me to this place—were mine. No one had forced me to pick up that gun, to rob that store, to live the life I had lived. I had made those choices, and now I had to face the consequences.

That realization was like a punch to the gut. For years, I had been living in denial, refusing to take responsibility for my actions. But prison has a way of stripping away the lies you tell yourself. It forces you to look in the mirror and see the truth, whether you like it or not.

At first, that truth was hard to swallow. I didn't want to believe that I was the reason I was here. It was easier to blame the system, to blame the streets, to blame anyone but myself. But the more I thought about it, the more I realized that I couldn't keep running from the truth.

I was responsible for my own life. And if I wanted to survive this, if I wanted to have any chance of finding a way out of the darkness, I had to take responsibility for the man I had become.

That was the first step. The first small step toward something different. I didn't know what that "something different" was yet, but I knew that I couldn't keep living the way I had been. The anger, the blame, the excuses—they were all chains holding me down, keeping me trapped in a cycle I couldn't escape.

But breaking those chains wasn't easy. The darkness inside me had been there for so long, it felt like a part of who I was. And even though I had started to see things differently, I still didn't know how to let go. I didn't know how to move forward.

Prison life continued around me, the same routine day after day. Wake up, eat, work, sleep. The monotony was suffocating, but in that monotony, I found space to think, to reflect. I started spending more time in the prison library, reading whatever I could get my hands on. Books became my escape, a way to occupy my mind and keep the darkness at bay. I read everything from novels to self-help books, anything that could help me make sense of what I was going through.

One book in particular stuck with me. It was about personal responsibility, about how we all have the power to choose our path, no matter where we come from or what we've been through. That book hit me like a ton of bricks. For so long, I had believed that my path was set and that I had no control over my life. But reading those words, I started to realize that maybe, just maybe, I had more power than I thought.

I started to see that change wasn't going to come from outside of me. It wasn't going to come from the system or the streets or anyone else. If I wanted to change, if I wanted to find a way out of the darkness, it had to come from within. I had to choose to be different, to live differently, even in a place as unforgiving as this.

It was a slow process. Change doesn't happen overnight, especially in a place like a prison. But little by little, I started to let go of the anger, the blame, the excuses. I started to take responsibility for my life, for my choices, for the man I had become.

Chapter 3

The Prison Code

When I first stepped into prison, I felt a wave of uncertainty wash over me. The clang of the cell doors echoed in my mind, a constant reminder of my new reality. I was no longer just Jamal from the streets—I was now an inmate, a number in a system that seemed designed to strip away identity and humanity. But I quickly learned that prison had its code, an unspoken set of rules that dictated how to survive, how to interact, and how to make it through each day without losing yourself.

The moment I entered my cell block, I was overwhelmed by the cacophony of voices, the scent of sweat and despair, and the sight of men who wore their scars like badges of honor. It was a place where vulnerability was a luxury few could afford. As I was led to my cell, I kept my head down, trying to blend in, but I could feel the eyes of the other inmates on me, sizing me up, searching for weakness. I was a new fish in a tank full of sharks.

The first week was an intense crash course in the prison code. I spent most of my time observing, watching how the men interacted, who seemed to command respect, and who was avoided like the plague. I learned quickly that respect was earned, not given, and the price for mistakes could be steep.

In the beginning, I avoided confrontation at all costs. I was terrified of what could happen if I stepped out of line. My instinct was to keep my head down, stay out of trouble, and learn the ropes. I observed the hierarchy that existed among the inmates—the power struggles, alliances, and betrayals that defined daily life.

Finding Allies

One day, while I was in the yard, I caught sight of a group of men playing basketball. I had always been good at the game, a talent that once brought me joy. I watched for a while, wishing I could join them but knowing I wasn't ready to put myself out there. But then one of the players, a tall guy named Kadeem, called me over.

"Yo, you want in?" he asked, a half-smile on his face.

My heart raced. This was a chance to show what I could do, but stepping onto the court also meant putting myself in the spotlight. I nodded, though I felt my stomach twist in knots.

The game was rough, but I held my own. With each point I scored, I felt a flicker of confidence ignite within me. Kadeem and his crew respected talent, and by the end of the game, I had earned a place among them.

"Not bad for a newbie," Kadeem said, slapping me on the back as we walked off the court. "Stick with us, and you'll be alright."

This was the first lesson of the prison code: find your tribe. In a place where betrayal could be lethal, having allies meant safety and security. I learned that forming connections was crucial, but I also had to be careful about whom I trusted.

Learning the Rules

As the days turned into weeks, I began to pick up on the nuances of prison life. I learned that certain words and actions held a weight that could shift the dynamics in an instant. The men here communicated with more than just words; it was about body language, eye contact, and the slightest gestures.

I witnessed how quickly a friendly conversation could turn into a confrontation. One afternoon, I saw a guy named Miguel get into a verbal spar with another inmate over a simple game of cards. What started as playful banter escalated into threats, and before I knew it, they were being pulled apart by the guards.

This was the reality of prison life—the tension was always simmering just below the surface, ready to boil over at any moment. I had to stay sharp, to know when to speak and when to remain silent.

The unwritten rules were everywhere. For example, I quickly learned that showing weakness was the quickest way to become a target. I kept my struggles to myself, refusing to let anyone see me break. Even during my darkest moments, I wore a mask of strength.

Respect and Fear

Respect in prison was a tricky balance between fear and admiration. I met a man named Tyrone who had a reputation as a tough guy. He was a force to be reckoned with, but he also had a sense of honor that set him apart. One day, while we were all sitting in the common area, he caught my eye and motioned for me to come over.

"You've been playing ball," he said, assessing me with a steady gaze. "You got skills. But remember, this place can eat you alive if you let it."

I nodded, feeling the weight of his words. "I'm just trying to stay out of trouble."

He chuckled, a deep, rumbling sound. "That's smart. But it's not enough. You gotta be ready to stand your ground. Don't let anyone push you around. You got something to prove, so prove it."

I took his advice to heart. The next time I was challenged over a game of cards, I held my ground. The other inmate was bigger than me, but I refused to back down. When I stood my ground, I felt a shift in how the others looked at me. I wasn't just another inmate; I was someone who could hold his own.

The Code of Survival

The prison code also involved a set of rules around the "do's and don'ts" of interactions. For example, never ask for favors without being prepared to pay them back. If you borrowed something, you better return it, or you risked losing face—or worse.

I learned to navigate these unwritten rules through observation and experience. I made it a point to help others when I could. If I had an extra pack of ramen, I'd share it with a fellow inmate who looked hungry. Small acts of kindness helped build my reputation as someone trustworthy.

But kindness in prison was a double-edged sword. It could open doors, but it could also make you vulnerable. I had to be careful not to appear too soft, or I risked being taken advantage of.

The Importance of Knowledge

Another crucial lesson I learned was the power of knowledge. In prison, information was currency. Knowing the right people, understanding the layout of the facility, and staying informed about the latest gossip could mean the difference between safety and danger.

I started reading everything I could get my hands on—books, magazines, anything that would give me insight into the world outside and the minds of the men I shared a cell with. I found solace in literature. Authors like Maya Angelou and James Baldwin spoke to my soul, and their words offered me a glimpse of hope.

As I absorbed their stories, I began to see how the lessons within those pages applied to my own life. I learned about resilience, strength, and the power of the human spirit. It was a revelation that would shape my path in unexpected ways.

Finding My Path

Despite the harsh realities, there were moments of camaraderie that reminded me of the humanity we all shared.

In the evenings, we'd gather in the yard, talking and sharing stories. I listened as the men recounted their lives before prison, the dreams they once had, and the mistakes that led them here. Each story was a piece of the larger puzzle of life behind bars.

I began to share my own story, how I got caught up in the wrong crowd, how my life spiraled out of control, and how I ended up here. It was cathartic, and I could see the impact my words had on others. They resonated with the struggles and choices that had led us all to this moment.

In those moments of vulnerability, I felt a sense of belonging. I was no longer just an inmate; I was part of a community, a brotherhood forged in the fires of shared experiences.

Turning Point

One fateful night, everything changed. There was a riot in the cell block—chaos erupted as tensions reached a boiling point. It felt like the walls themselves were shaking as the shouts and screams echoed through the halls.

I remember standing in my cell, heart racing, not knowing whether to run or stay put. In that moment, I saw the reality of what prison life could become—a fight for survival.

But amid the chaos, I remembered Tyrone's words: "Stand your ground." I stepped out of my cell, the adrenaline coursing through my veins. I couldn't just be another victim in this place; I had to take control of my fate.

As I moved through the corridors, I saw men fighting, throwing punches, and the guards struggling to maintain order. I spotted Kadeem in the fray, and instinct kicked in. I rushed over to him, ready to help.

"Jamal! What are you doing?" he shouted amidst the chaos.

"Just trying to keep it from getting worse!" I yelled back, adrenaline pumping through my veins.

Together, we grabbed a couple of other inmates and formed a human barrier, trying to break up the fights. It was terrifying, but it was also exhilarating. In that moment, I felt alive—like I was finally becoming the man I needed to be.

Aftermath and Reflection

When the dust finally settled, I stood panting, my heart racing, and I realized that I had crossed a line. I had stepped up, faced my fears, and taken control in a situation that could have easily spiraled out of control.

In the aftermath of the riot, I could feel a shift among the inmates. I had earned respect in a way I hadn't anticipated. The other men saw that I was willing to fight for my survival, and I could see their acknowledgment in their eyes.

But the experience also left me shaken. The violence, the chaos—it was a reminder of how quickly things could change in prison. I had survived this time, but what about the next? I knew I had to be vigilant, to continue navigating the prison code with care.

Building My Identity

As the weeks turned into months, I began to carve out an identity for myself within these walls. I was no longer just a number; I was Jamal—a man who had learned the rules and was determined to live by them. I found purpose in mentoring other new inmates, sharing the lessons I had learned about survival and the importance of community.

I had come to understand that while the prison code was essential for survival, it was the connections I built and the knowledge I gained that would ultimately help me transform my life. I was no longer just a prisoner; I was a part of something bigger.

I spent hours discussing life with my fellow inmates, encouraging them to find their purpose even within these walls. I learned that even in the darkest places, there were glimmers of hope, and my job was to help others see that light.

Preparing for the Future

As I continued to navigate this complex world, I began to think about what life would look like once I got out. I knew I couldn't stay in this mindset forever, and I was determined to find a way to break free from the cycle of violence and despair.

I spent my days dreaming of a future where I could take my experiences and use them to help others outside these walls. I started writing again, documenting my thoughts, reflections, and the lessons I had learned.

It was a way to process my experiences and prepare myself for the life that awaited me on the other side.

I thought about the legacy I wanted to leave behind—one built on resilience, hope, and the power of choice. I was determined to show others that even in the darkest moments, there was a way out.

Conclusion

The prison code taught me invaluable lessons about survival, respect, and the importance of community. I learned that while I had to be tough to survive, I also had to be compassionate and willing to help others along the way.

As I navigated this new world, I began to realize that my experiences were shaping me into the man I was meant to be. I was no longer just a product of my environment; I was becoming an agent of change, ready to make a difference—both inside these walls and beyond them.

Chapter 4

A Glimmer of Hope

The air in prison is heavy with despair, a weight that hangs over every soul trapped within its walls. But amidst that darkness, hope can be a flicker—a small light that dares to shine against the odds. My journey through the early days of incarceration had been marked by fear, survival, and learning the unspoken code of the prison yard. Little did I know that a simple encounter would begin to change the course of my life.

The Encounter with Mr. Jenkins

It was an ordinary day in the common area. The buzz of conversation filled the room as inmates gathered for their daily dose of sun and interaction. Most were playing cards or talking about their lives outside these walls, but I found myself sitting alone, lost in thought. I was still grappling with the events of the riot, the fear and adrenaline still fresh in my mind.

As I sat quietly, I noticed an older man sitting across the room. He had a calm demeanor, with a beard that looked as if it had seen its fair share of grey hairs. He was reading a book, completely absorbed. There was something about him—an aura of wisdom that drew me in.

I had seen him before but had never spoken to him. His name was Mr. Jenkins, and he was a lifer, serving time for a crime that had taken place decades ago. Despite his situation, he seemed at peace, an anomaly in a place where chaos reigned. Something compelled me to approach him.

"Hey, what are you reading?" I asked, trying to sound casual.

He looked up from his book, a gentle smile spreading across his face. "It's a collection of poems by Langston Hughes. Would you like to join me?"

I hesitated for a moment, unsure if I should take a seat. But there was a warmth in his invitation, so I nodded and sat down. "I've never really read poetry before," I admitted.

"Poetry is the voice of the soul," he replied, his eyes sparkling with enthusiasm. "It's a way to express what we feel inside, especially in a place like this."

His words resonated with me. I had never thought of poetry as anything more than words on a page, but the way he spoke about it made me curious. "Can you share some?" I asked.

He nodded, flipping through the pages until he found a piece that struck him. As he read aloud, I felt a connection to the words. They spoke of struggle, resilience, and the unwavering spirit of humanity. It was a glimpse into a world where hope flourished even in the bleakest of circumstances.

The Seed of Change

Over the next few weeks, I began to spend more time with Mr. Jenkins. He introduced me to the world of literature, sharing his favorite authors and poets.

Each conversation felt like a revelation, opening my eyes to new perspectives and ideas. He became a mentor, guiding me through the maze of my thoughts and emotions.

"Jamal, what do you want out of this experience?" he asked one day as we sat under the flickering fluorescent lights of the common area.

I paused, contemplating his question. "I don't know, man. I just want to get out of here and forget all this. I want to be someone again."

"Then start with who you are now," he replied. "You can't change your past, but you can shape your future. Use this time to become the man you want to be."

His words struck a chord within me. I realized that I had been so focused on survival that I had neglected to think about what came next. What would I do when I left this place? What kind of man did I want to be?

It was time for a change, and it had to start within. I began to pour myself into the books Mr. Jenkins suggested, finding solace and inspiration in their pages. The words ignited a fire in me—a desire to learn, to grow, and to redefine my purpose.

The Power of Education

Motivated by Mr. Jenkins, I enrolled in a few educational programs offered within the prison. It was a challenging decision; many of my fellow inmates scoffed at the idea of education, thinking it was a waste of time.

But I was done allowing others to dictate my path. I was determined to break the cycle and build a future for myself.

The classes were a mix of subjects—math, literature, and even vocational skills. I found myself in a classroom for the first time in years, and it felt surreal. The feeling of learning something new awakened parts of me that I thought had long been buried.

Each lesson brought me closer to understanding myself. I discovered a passion for writing that I never knew existed. The words flowed from my pen like a river, capturing my thoughts, experiences, and dreams for the future. I wrote about my struggles, my fears, and the lessons I had learned. Writing became my lifeline, a way to process everything that had happened, and a means of escape from the confines of my reality.

As I delved deeper into my studies, I found a sense of community among my classmates. We were all searching for something—redemption, understanding, a way out. Our discussions were raw and honest, often diving into the realities of our pasts and the hopes for our futures. In those moments, I realized I wasn't alone. We were all on a journey, each of us fighting our own battles.

Connecting with Others

One afternoon, after a particularly inspiring class, I decided to organize a poetry reading among the inmates. I wanted to create a space where we could share our stories, express ourselves, and uplift one another. The idea was met with skepticism at first, but as I spoke passionately about the power of words, I began to see interest spark in their eyes.

"Why not?" one of the guys said, a hint of a smile breaking through his hardened exterior. "Let's give it a shot."

That night, we gathered in the common area, a motley crew of inmates from different backgrounds and experiences. Some were seasoned poets, while others had never shared their thoughts aloud. But as the night progressed, something magical happened.

With each poem recited, barriers broke down. Laughter mixed with tears as we shared our stories, revealing the vulnerabilities we had hidden for so long. It was cathartic, and the energy in the room was palpable. I realized that through our shared experiences, we were beginning to heal.

A Lesson in Empathy

As I listened to my fellow inmates share their struggles, I began to understand the depth of their pain. Many of them had faced challenges I could only imagine—loss, addiction, betrayal. Their stories mirrored my own, and I felt an overwhelming sense of empathy.

At that moment, I knew that I wasn't just writing for myself anymore; I was writing for them too. I wanted my words to resonate beyond the walls of our prison, to reach others who felt lost and hopeless. I began to write pieces that spoke of resilience and hope, capturing the essence of our shared experiences.

With Mr. Jenkins as my guide, I honed my skills, crafting poems that spoke of the struggles we faced and the glimmers of hope we could find amidst the darkness. Each word became a testament to our resilience, a reminder that we were more than our mistakes.

A Turning Point

As I continued to write and connect with others, I started to see a change in myself. I was no longer just surviving; I was living. The flicker of hope that had begun with my conversations with Mr. Jenkins transformed into a flame, lighting my path forward.

But just as I began to feel a sense of stability, I was reminded that life in prison was unpredictable. One day, during a routine check, I learned that a lockdown had been initiated due to a fight in another cell block. Tensions ran high, and the atmosphere shifted dramatically.

The guards were on edge, and we were confined to our cells for hours, the sounds of chaos echoing in the distance. I lay on my bunk, staring at the ceiling, grappling with the fear that gripped my heart. I thought about everything I had learned, the progress I had made, and the purpose I had begun to find. What if it all came crashing down?

Rediscovering Faith

Amid that uncertainty, I felt a deep yearning for guidance. I turned to the writings of poets like Langston Hughes and Maya Angelou, searching for solace in their words.

I realized that they had faced their struggles and had emerged stronger on the other side. Their resilience fueled my determination to keep going.

I picked up my pen and began to write again, pouring my heart into my journal. I wrote about my fears, my dreams, and the glimmers of hope that still shone through the cracks of despair. Each word was a reminder that I was not defined by my circumstances, but by how I chose to respond to them.

As the lockdown continued, I felt a shift within me. I began to pray, something I hadn't done in years. I sought strength and guidance, hoping to find clarity amidst the chaos.

Emerging Stronger

Eventually, the lockdown ended, and life resumed its chaotic rhythm. But I emerged from that experience stronger and more determined than ever. I had faced fear head-on and found my voice in the process. The flicker of hope had transformed into a burning desire to forge a new path.

I returned to my poetry group with renewed energy. I shared my experiences during the lockdown, and my fellow inmates resonated with my words. It became a catalyst for deeper conversations about fear, resilience, and the power of hope.

Through poetry, we began to dream together—about our lives after prison, the families we wanted to reunite with, and the changes we hoped to make. Each story shared was a brick in the foundation of our newfound camaraderie.

Conclusion: The Road Ahead

As I reflected on the events of that chapter of my life, I understood that hope is a powerful force. It can arise from the unlikeliest of places and can ignite the spark of change within even the most desolate situations.

My journey through prison had only just begun, but I was no longer afraid of the challenges that lay ahead. With the support of my fellow inmates and the guidance of mentors like Mr. Jenkins, I felt ready to face whatever came my way.

Little did I know that the glimmer of hope I had discovered would become the beacon that guided me through the darkest of nights, lighting the path to a future I once thought impossible.

Chapter 5

Finding Purpose Behind Bars

Prison is often viewed as a place of confinement, a dark abyss where hope seems to vanish. Yet, within its walls, I began to understand that it could also be a space for profound personal growth and transformation. As I immersed myself in literature, forged connections with my fellow inmates, and engaged in the educational programs offered, I discovered a renewed sense of purpose that would guide me through the darkest days of my incarceration.

A Shift in Perspective

The more time I spent with Mr. Jenkins and my fellow inmates, the more I realized that each of us had a story, a journey that led us to this place. While our pasts were riddled with mistakes and regrets, they also held the potential for redemption. This understanding sparked something within me—a desire not just to survive but to thrive and help others in the process.

In our poetry group, we began to explore the idea of purpose. What did it mean to have a purpose in a place like this? Many of my peers had long ago given up on the idea of a future, resigned to the belief that their lives would be defined by their time behind bars. But I knew that change was possible, and I wanted to prove it—not just to myself but to everyone around me.

The Birth of the Writing Workshop

With my newfound perspective, I decided to take action. Inspired by the poetry readings we held, I proposed starting a writing workshop for inmates. I envisioned a space where we could explore our thoughts and emotions through writing, creating a community of support and creativity.

At first, the idea was met with skepticism. "What's the point?" some of the guys said. "We're just going to be here forever." But I pressed on, sharing my own experiences of how writing had helped me process my feelings and envision a different future. Gradually, I began to see interest ignite in their eyes.

Finally, with the approval of the prison administration, the writing workshop became a reality. We gathered in a small, dimly lit room, a motley crew of inmates from various backgrounds, each carrying the weight of their pasts. I was nervous but excited, eager to see how our stories would unfold.

The First Session: Breaking the Ice

During our first session, I introduced the concept of free writing—an exercise where we would write without judgment, allowing our thoughts to flow freely onto the page. I encouraged everyone to share their writing if they felt comfortable, emphasizing that there were no wrong answers and no judgments here.

As we began to write, I watched as the atmosphere shifted. The tension in the room eased, and a sense of camaraderie began to develop. I could see that many of the men were struggling to find their voice, but as they scribbled their thoughts, it became evident that they were searching for a way to express themselves.

When it was time to share, a hesitant inmate named Marcus spoke up. "I don't know how to write," he admitted, his voice barely above a whisper. "But I'll try."

He read a few lines that spoke of his regrets and the pain he felt for his family. As he spoke, I could see the vulnerability in his eyes—the struggle to articulate his feelings in a world that often forced us to suppress them. When he finished, there was a moment of silence before a round of applause erupted. It was a simple acknowledgment, but it was powerful.

One by one, others began to share. The workshop became a safe space where we could drop our guards and allow ourselves to be vulnerable. We wrote about our families, our dreams, and the mistakes we had made.

Finding Common Ground

As the weeks progressed, I noticed a transformation in the group. The men began to open up, sharing not only their writing but their lives. It was a remarkable experience to witness, as we found common ground in our struggles. Despite our different backgrounds, we all shared a common humanity.

The writing workshop was more than just a creative outlet; it became a source of healing. We would sit in a circle, sharing our pieces and offering support. Each story we shared was a reminder that we were not alone in our struggles.

One day, a quiet inmate named Leon, who had always kept to himself, read a piece that moved everyone to tears. He spoke of his childhood, the loss of his father, and how he had turned to crime as a means of survival. His raw honesty resonated with all of us, and in that moment, the walls between us crumbled.

"I never thought I could share this," he said, wiping tears from his eyes. "But writing helped me see my pain in a different light."

His words sparked a conversation about vulnerability and the importance of expressing our emotions. It was a turning point for the group, as we all began to realize that our experiences, no matter how painful, could catalyze change.

Building a Community

As our workshop continued, I became more determined to create a sense of community among the inmates. We decided to organize an open mic night, where we could showcase our writing and invite other inmates to join us. It was a daunting task, but I believed it would foster a sense of belonging and purpose.

The night of the open mic, the energy in the room was electric. Inmates from different blocks gathered to hear the stories we had written.

I felt a surge of pride as I watched my peers step up to the mic, sharing their poems and essays with a sense of confidence that hadn't existed before.

One of the highlights of the night came when a fellow inmate named Chris, known for his tough exterior, took the stage. As he began to read, his voice trembled, but he pushed through, revealing a poignant piece about love and loss. The room fell silent, captivated by his vulnerability.

When he finished, the audience erupted in applause. Chris's eyes were wide with disbelief; he had found a voice he never knew he had. The moment marked a significant shift—not just for him, but for all of us. We were learning that our words had the power to impact others, to inspire change, and to create connections.

Embracing Change

With each workshop and event, I could feel the atmosphere in the prison shifting. Inmates were beginning to find their purpose, their voices, and a sense of hope. It was as if the act of writing had opened a door to self-discovery and healing.

Encouraged by the positive response, I began to expand our writing program. I reached out to local authors and poets, inviting them to come and share their experiences with us. Their visits brought new energy to our group, inspiring us to reach even deeper within ourselves.

I also connected with a nonprofit organization that provided writing resources for incarcerated individuals. They agreed to send us books and materials, which only fueled our passion for learning and growth. Each new resource felt like a lifeline, a reminder that we were not forgotten.

The Turning Point: A Letter of Encouragement

As my commitment to the writing workshop grew, so did my desire to help others who were struggling with their circumstances. One day, I decided to write letters to some of my fellow inmates who were dealing with isolation and depression. I wanted them to know they weren't alone, that there was still hope.

In my letters, I shared my journey, the struggles I had faced, and how writing had helped me find purpose. I encouraged them to join our workshop and express themselves through words.

To my surprise, I received heartfelt responses. Some of the men wrote back, sharing their own stories of pain and longing. They expressed gratitude for my encouragement, and slowly, they began to join our workshops, seeking solace and connection.

The Ripple Effect

As our writing community continued to grow, I began to witness the ripple effect of our efforts. More inmates were stepping out of their shells, sharing their stories, and supporting one another. The environment in our unit shifted from one of fear and distrust to one of camaraderie and support.

We held themed writing challenges, encouraging everyone to write about their hopes for the future, their dreams, and their aspirations. The creativity that flowed from our group was astounding; we were no longer defined by our past mistakes but by our ability to envision a brighter future.

During one session, a fellow inmate named Darnell shared a piece that captured the essence of our collective journey. His words were raw and powerful, reflecting the pain of incarceration but also the hope that had begun to flourish within us.

"I used to think this place would break me," he said, his voice steady. "But through writing, I've found a way to heal. We're more than our mistakes—we're warriors."

A Vision for the Future

As I reflected on the progress we had made, I felt a sense of pride. The writing workshop had become a lifeline for so many, offering not just a creative outlet but a sense of purpose. It was a space where we could be ourselves, explore our emotions, and support one another.

With the newfound confidence and unity among us, I began to envision a future where our voices could reach beyond the prison walls. I wanted to compile our stories into a book, a collection of our writings that would showcase the resilience of our spirits.

I shared my idea with the group, and to my delight, they embraced it with enthusiasm.

We set a goal to complete our manuscript by the end of the year, determined to capture the essence of our journey and the power of words.

Conclusion: The Power of Purpose

Finding purpose behind bars transformed my life in ways I never could have imagined. Through writing, I discovered not only my voice but also the voices of those around me. We were no longer just inmates; we were a community bonded by our shared experiences and a commitment to growth.

As I continued to navigate the challenges of prison life, I felt empowered by the knowledge that I was making a difference, not just for myself but for those who would follow in my footsteps. The journey wasn't easy, but it was necessary. I was ready to embrace the challenges ahead, armed with the belief that purpose could be found even in the darkest of places.

Little did I know, this was just the beginning of a journey that would lead me to heights I had never dreamed possible.

Chapter 6

Redemption in the Smallest Acts

As I settled into a routine within the prison walls, I started to grasp the profound truth that redemption is often found in the smallest acts. While it was tempting to think of monumental changes as the only path to transformation, I began to realize that true growth came from consistent, intentional actions—both big and small.

Understanding Redemption

The word "redemption" often conjures up images of grand gestures or dramatic transformations. But as I continued to navigate my life behind bars, I came to understand that redemption could also be about the little things—the choices we make each day, the kindness we extend to others, and the ability to rise above our circumstances.

Every morning, I would wake up in my small cell, a place that once felt like a prison in the literal sense and now began to feel like an opportunity for growth. Each day was a blank slate, a chance to make choices that would either lead me closer to redemption or further away from it.

Acts of Kindness

One of the first small acts I engaged in was offering to help fellow inmates with their reading and writing skills. Many of the men around me struggled with literacy, often hiding their difficulties out of shame. One day, I noticed a man named Terry, who was sitting alone in the yard, looking dejected as he fumbled through a book. I approached him, and with a friendly smile, asked if he wanted help.

At first, he hesitated. "I'm not really good at this," he said, his eyes downcast. But I reassured him that it was okay to struggle and that we could work together. Over the next few weeks, we met regularly, and I watched as he transformed from a hesitant reader into someone who could tackle complex material.

Terry's confidence began to grow, and soon he was reading poetry aloud to the group during our writing sessions. His transformation inspired others to seek help as well, and it was during those moments of tutoring that I found my own sense of purpose.

Leading by Example

As I continued to help others, I realized that my own behavior was equally important. I had to embody the change I wanted to see in myself and in my community. This meant being mindful of how I interacted with everyone around me, whether it was through offering a listening ear or simply being respectful, even in the most challenging situations.

One day, I witnessed a heated argument between two inmates, each determined to prove their point. As tensions escalated, I intervened, calmly suggesting they take a moment to breathe and step back from the confrontation. I shared a simple phrase that had become my mantra: "We can either be a part of the problem or a part of the solution."

Surprisingly, they took my advice and separated for a few moments. When they returned, they were more composed, and a meaningful conversation followed. It was a small victory, but I realized that being a peacemaker in a chaotic environment was a step toward my own redemption.

Self-Control and Growth

The journey to redemption also required me to confront my own triggers and learn self-control. In the beginning, I struggled with anger. Memories of my past and the injustices I faced often resurfaced, igniting a fire within me. But I began to understand that responding with anger wouldn't change my circumstances—it would only perpetuate a cycle of violence and resentment.

I sought guidance from the prison chaplain, a wise man who had dedicated his life to helping others find their way. He taught me mindfulness techniques and meditation practices that helped me manage my emotions. During our sessions, I learned to pause before reacting, to consider the consequences of my actions.

One day, while waiting in line for lunch, I found myself growing irritated with an inmate who was pushing ahead. Instead of lashing out, I took a deep breath and reminded myself of the lessons I had learned. I calmly addressed him, explaining how it felt to be pushed aside. To my surprise, he apologized and stepped back. That moment was empowering, reinforcing the idea that redemption often lies in our ability to choose peace over conflict.

The Impact of Small Changes

As I continued to embrace small acts of kindness and self-control, I noticed a ripple effect in my surroundings. Other inmates began to emulate my behavior. They too started helping one another, whether it was sharing food, offering advice, or simply listening. The atmosphere in our unit shifted from one of competition and hostility to one of support and camaraderie.

During one workshop session, I shared my observations about how small changes could lead to significant transformations. I encouraged everyone to think of one small act they could commit to that week—whether it was helping another inmate with a task or choosing to respond calmly in a tense situation.

To my delight, the responses were overwhelming. Inmates shared their commitments: one would start a weekly game night to bring others together; another decided to mentor younger inmates on how to navigate prison life. Each pledge was a testament to the power of redemption in the smallest acts.

Facing Challenges Together

Despite the progress we had made, challenges still arose. Conflicts and misunderstandings were inevitable in such a confined space. But instead of reverting to old habits, we began to face these challenges together. We held discussions about our grievances, offering one another support and guidance.

One day, a serious incident erupted between two inmates from rival neighborhoods. It could have easily escalated into violence, but instead, I called for a meeting. I gathered the interested parties, along with a few others from our writing group, and we talked it out. We didn't shy away from the anger and hurt; we acknowledged it and worked toward understanding.

During the discussion, it became clear that both sides were operating from a place of pain. By the end of the meeting, we reached a consensus: instead of allowing our pasts to dictate our actions, we would commit to being better. It was another small act of redemption, but it felt monumental at that moment.

Personal Reflection: The Journey of Redemption

As I reflected on my own journey, I realized that redemption is not a destination but a continuous journey. It requires constant vigilance and a willingness to confront our flaws. I recognized that each act of kindness I extended to others was also a gift to myself, a way of nurturing my growth.

Through helping others, I found healing for my own wounds. I was no longer just a product of my past but a participant in shaping a brighter future—for myself and for those around me. Every moment spent nurturing relationships and fostering a sense of community was a step toward redemption.

The Power of Forgiveness

One of the most profound lessons I learned during this chapter of my life was the importance of forgiveness. In a place where anger and resentment could fester, I understood that holding onto grudges only hindered our growth. It took time, but I began to let go of the pain I had been carrying—pain from my past, pain inflicted by others, and pain I had caused myself.

One day, I sat in my cell, writing a letter to my mother, who had suffered because of my choices. I expressed my regret for the hurt I caused her and sought her forgiveness. As I poured my heart out onto the pages, I felt a weight lift off my shoulders.

When I finally received her response, I could sense her love and understanding. It wasn't just a letter; it was a bridge back to the love we once shared. Forgiveness is powerful, and it taught me that while I could not change my past, I could shape my future.

Conclusion: The Journey Continues

As I moved forward, I knew that redemption wasn't an end goal but an ongoing journey. Every small act of kindness, every moment of self-control, and every opportunity to uplift others was a stepping stone toward a better life.

I felt a deep sense of gratitude for the lessons I had learned and the relationships I had forged. The prison walls, once symbols of confinement, began to feel like a backdrop for a transformative journey.

With each passing day, I was becoming a better version of myself—not just for me, but for the community around me. I realized that my story of redemption could inspire others to embark on their own journeys of growth, and that thought alone filled me with hope.

Little did I know, this chapter would lay the groundwork for the changes to come as I faced the most significant challenge of my life: the journey toward freedom.

Chapter 7

Facing the Outside World

As I stood at the gates of the prison, a wave of emotions washed over me—excitement, fear, hope, and uncertainty all blended into one. After years of confinement, the prospect of freedom was exhilarating yet daunting. I was finally free, yet the world outside seemed like an uncharted territory filled with both opportunity and peril.

The Moment of Release

The morning sun shone brightly as I walked out of the prison gates. I could feel the warmth on my skin, a stark contrast to the cold, sterile walls I had known for so long. I took a deep breath, inhaling the fresh air as if I were tasting freedom for the first time. It was a surreal moment; I had dreamt of this day for years, yet standing here felt like stepping into a dream—a reality that was both thrilling and terrifying.

As I walked towards the waiting area, my mind raced with thoughts of what lay ahead. The world outside had changed in ways I couldn't comprehend. What would people think of me? Would I be accepted, or would I face the same rejection I had experienced before? My heart pounded in my chest, a reminder that freedom came with its own set of challenges.

The First Encounter

When I stepped into the waiting area, I was greeted by a familiar face—my older brother, Marcus. He had been my rock through the years, visiting me regularly and supporting me throughout my journey in prison. As he rushed toward me with a big smile, I felt a sense of comfort wash over me.

"Man, it's so good to see you!" he exclaimed, pulling me into a tight hug. "Welcome home!"

"Thanks, bro. It feels surreal," I replied, feeling both grateful and overwhelmed.

We stood outside for a moment, taking in the sights and sounds of the bustling street. Cars zoomed past, people walked briskly, and the distant sounds of laughter filled the air. It was a cacophony I had missed, yet it felt foreign.

"Ready to face the world?" Marcus asked, a mix of encouragement and caution in his voice.

I nodded, though doubt lingered in my mind. "Yeah, I guess so."

Rebuilding Connections

In the weeks that followed, I tried to acclimate to life outside prison. Marcus took me in, providing a stable home environment and a sense of normalcy. I quickly realized that reconnecting with family and friends was essential. My mother had always been my anchor, and as I reached out to her, I felt a mix of excitement and fear about how our relationship had changed.

The first time I spoke to her after my release was emotional. When I entered her house, the familiar scents of home flooded my senses. She was in the kitchen, baking her famous cornbread, and when she saw me, her eyes welled up with tears.

"Oh, my baby! You're home!" she cried, enveloping me in a warm embrace.

"Hi, Mom. I missed you," I said, fighting back tears of my own.

We spent hours talking, sharing stories about my time in prison and her life while I was away. The distance of the years melted away as we laughed and cried together, but I couldn't help but feel the weight of my past hanging between us.

Facing the Judgment

While reconnecting with family was uplifting, facing the outside world brought its challenges. I quickly learned that the stigma of being an ex-convict was hard to shake off. When I ventured into the community, I could feel the judgment in people's eyes—the whispers, the sideways glances.

One afternoon, I went to a local café to grab a coffee. As I stood in line, I overheard a conversation between two patrons.

"Did you hear he just got out of prison?" one said, her voice dripping with disdain.

"I can't believe they let him back out. People like that never change," her friend replied.

I felt the heat rising to my cheeks, and for a moment, I considered leaving. But I reminded myself of the progress I had made in prison and the lessons I had learned. This was part of my new reality, and I couldn't allow the opinions of others to dictate my worth.

Job Hunting: A New Challenge

With the support of Marcus and my mother, I began searching for a job. I had aspirations of finding meaningful work, but the reality of being a felon made it challenging. Each application I submitted came with a weight of uncertainty.

I was determined to stay positive, so I reached out to organizations that focused on helping ex-offenders reintegrate into society. I attended job fairs and workshops, learning how to present myself confidently and address my past honestly.

The first few interviews were daunting. I practiced my responses, rehearsing how to explain my absence from the workforce without allowing it to overshadow my qualifications. During one interview, I encountered a friendly but skeptical employer.

"Your experience is impressive, but you have to understand that your past raises concerns," he said.

"I know," I replied, my heart racing. "But I can assure you that I've changed. I'm committed to making better choices moving forward. I want to prove that I'm capable of being a valuable asset to your team."

While I didn't land the job, I left the interview feeling proud of myself for facing the challenge head-on. Each experience, whether successful or not, taught me resilience and strengthened my resolve.

The Temptation to Revert

Despite my best efforts to stay focused on my goals, the temptation to revert to my old ways lingered. There were moments of weakness—frustration when job hunting became overwhelming, memories of my past life calling out to me. I had to confront the truth: the streets I once roamed still existed, and the pull of familiar habits was strong.

One evening, I found myself walking through my old neighborhood, nostalgia washing over me like a wave. The laughter of old friends echoed in my ears, and I felt the familiar tug of the life I had left behind. I could easily slip back into that world, but I had come too far to let temptation dictate my path.

I called Marcus, who could sense my internal struggle. "You're stronger than this, bro," he said. "You've worked hard to get here. Don't let your past define your future."

His words were a reminder of the purpose I had found in prison, the transformation I had undergone. I decided to redirect my energy into positive outlets—volunteering at a local community center, mentoring young men, and sharing my story with those who needed encouragement.

Creating a New Support System

Building a new support system became essential in navigating my newfound freedom. I sought out groups of individuals who had similar experiences and those who understood the complexities of reintegrating into society. I attended support meetings and connected with others who had faced the same challenges.

In one of those meetings, I met David, a man in his thirties who had also recently been released from prison. We quickly bonded over our shared experiences, and I found comfort in our conversations.

"Man, it's tough out here," he admitted one evening. "But we can't let it defeat us."

"Exactly," I replied. "We've come too far to go back. Let's hold each other accountable."

We became each other's cheerleaders, celebrating small victories and offering support during setbacks. Together, we attended job fairs and workshops, encouraging one another to keep pushing forward despite the obstacles.

A Turning Point

As I continued my journey, I finally landed a job at a local nonprofit organization dedicated to helping at-risk youth. I was thrilled to contribute to a cause I believed in, and it felt like a perfect fit. In my role, I facilitated workshops that focused on personal development, resilience, and the power of choice.

On my first day, I stood in front of a group of eager young faces, sharing my story of redemption. "I know what it feels like to be lost," I began, "but I also know what it takes to find your way back. You have the power to change your narrative."

As I spoke, I could see the light of hope flicker in their eyes. This was what I was meant to do—help others see that they could rise above their circumstances, just as I had.

Reflection: Embracing the Journey

Each day brought new challenges, but I faced them with a renewed sense of purpose. I was learning to embrace the journey, understanding that it wasn't just about the destination but the experiences and growth along the way.

As I navigated life outside of prison, I often reflected on the lessons I had learned during my time behind bars. The small acts of kindness, the struggles for self-control, and the importance of community had all played a significant role in shaping who I was becoming.

While I still faced obstacles and moments of doubt, I recognized that I had the strength to overcome them. I was no longer defined by my past but empowered by my choices.

Conclusion: The Road Ahead

As I looked to the future, I knew that the road ahead would not always be easy. I would continue to face judgment, setbacks, and temptations. But I was ready. I had built a foundation of resilience and hope, and I was determined to walk the path of purpose.

Facing the outside world was a challenge, but it was one I was willing to embrace. With the support of my brother, my family, and my newfound community, I knew that I could create a life filled with meaning and impact.

Chapter 8

Walking the Path of Purpose

The morning after my first day at the nonprofit felt different; it was as if the sun had risen with a new purpose. I had spent years dreaming of a life where I could make a difference, and now I was finally on that path. But the journey ahead was still filled with uncertainty. Each day brought new challenges, yet the drive to create a better life for myself and those around me pushed me forward.

A New Beginning

My first few weeks at the nonprofit were a whirlwind of activity. I met dedicated individuals who were passionate about making a positive impact in the community. We worked tirelessly, planning workshops, organizing events, and engaging with the youth we aimed to support. I was invigorated by the shared vision of change, and every moment felt like a step closer to fulfilling my purpose.

One of my primary responsibilities was leading a weekly workshop focused on resilience and personal growth. I poured my heart into developing the curriculum, drawing from my own experiences. Each session was an opportunity to connect with the young men and women who attended, to share my story of transformation, and to inspire them to pursue their paths.

As I stood in front of the group for the first session, a wave of nerves washed over me. "Hey everyone, I'm Jamal," I introduced myself, feeling the weight of their eyes on me. "I'm here to share my story, but more importantly, I want to hear yours."

I started by recounting my journey, the mistakes I had made, and the lessons I learned. The more I spoke, the more I saw their expressions shift from skepticism to interest. By the end of the session, several participants approached me with questions and stories of their own. In those moments, I felt a sense of purpose ignite within me.

Building Relationships

Over time, I developed meaningful relationships with many of the young people who attended my workshops. They came from various backgrounds, each with their struggles and aspirations. I listened to their stories, shared my insights, and offered support wherever I could.

One young man, Jamal, particularly struck me. He was bright and full of potential but was caught up in the wrong crowd. During one of our sessions, he confided in me about the pressure he felt to conform and the fear of stepping away from his friends.

"I don't want to disappoint them, but I know it's not the right path," he said, his voice filled with frustration.

"Jamal, I get it. I was there once too. But true friends will support your growth. You have to choose what's best for you,"

I encouraged him. "It's about breaking the cycle and creating a future you're proud of."

As he opened up, I saw a flicker of hope in his eyes. He started to attend my workshops regularly, and slowly but surely, he began to shift his mindset.

Challenging Myself

While my work was fulfilling, I recognized the importance of challenging myself outside of the nonprofit. I signed up for courses at a local community college, determined to further my education and equip myself with skills that would enhance my ability to help others.

The first day of class was nerve-wracking. I walked into the classroom filled with students who seemed much younger and more confident than I felt. I sat down, trying to calm my racing heart.

As the instructor began, I realized that this was another opportunity to learn and grow. The subjects fascinated me, and I found myself immersed in the material. I would study late into the night, driven by the desire to make the most of this chance.

The more I learned, the more I wanted to share with the young people I worked with. I incorporated new ideas into my workshops, emphasizing the importance of education and self-improvement.

A Setback and a Lesson

Despite my progress, life had a way of reminding me that the path to purpose was not always smooth. One evening, as I returned home from a late class, I was confronted by a group of familiar faces from my past.

"Look who it is! The 'changed man,'" one of them sneered. The others laughed, their eyes filled with mockery.

I felt my heart race, the memories of my past flooding back. They were right—there I was, standing before them, a reminder of the life I had once led. The temptation to engage in their banter tugged at me. I could easily slip back into that persona, but I fought to hold my ground.

"Yeah, I've changed," I replied firmly. "And I'm not going back."

Their laughter faded, replaced by an uneasy silence. I felt their eyes on me, judging but also surprised. It was a pivotal moment, one that reminded me of the strength I had gained in my journey.

Finding My Voice

Empowered by that encounter, I became more vocal about my mission and the importance of choosing a different path. I started a blog to share my journey and insights, hoping to reach a broader audience beyond the nonprofit. Writing became a therapeutic outlet, allowing me to process my experiences while inspiring others who might find themselves in similar situations.

I shared stories of resilience, lessons learned, and tips for overcoming obstacles. The feedback was overwhelming. Many readers reached out, expressing gratitude for my honesty and encouragement. It was then that I realized the power of storytelling and how it could forge connections.

Community Engagement

As my blog gained traction, I received an invitation to speak at a community event. The thought of speaking in front of a crowd both excited and terrified me. But I knew this was an opportunity to spread my message further.

On the day of the event, I stood backstage, feeling the weight of my purpose. When it was finally my turn to speak, I took a deep breath and stepped into the spotlight.

"Thank you for having me," I began, my voice steady despite the nerves. "I want to share my story, but more importantly, I want to encourage you to chase your dreams, no matter how far they may seem."

As I spoke, I saw the faces in the audience light up with understanding and empathy. I shared my struggles and triumphs, emphasizing the importance of resilience and community support.

When I finished, the applause was deafening, and I felt a rush of gratitude. I realized I wasn't just sharing my story; I was igniting hope in others, showing them that change was possible.

Giving Back

Motivated by my experiences, I decided to initiate a mentorship program through the nonprofit. I envisioned a space where young people could connect with mentors who had walked similar paths. The goal was to provide guidance, support, and encouragement as they navigated their journeys.

I worked tirelessly to recruit mentors and organize workshops. The program launched with great success, attracting a diverse group of participants eager to learn and grow. It was incredible to see the connections forming between mentors and mentees, and I knew we were making a meaningful impact in the community.

During one workshop, I watched as Jamal confidently shared his goals and aspirations with the group. I felt a swell of pride knowing I had played a part in his growth.

Celebrating Progress

As the months passed, I continued to witness transformation in myself and the young people I worked with. Their stories became intertwined with mine, a tapestry of resilience and hope.

At the end of the year, we organized a celebration to showcase the achievements of our mentees. Families, friends, and community members gathered to honor their progress. It was a beautiful evening filled with laughter, tears, and inspiring stories.

When it was my turn to speak, I looked out at the crowd and felt an overwhelming sense of gratitude. "This is what purpose looks like," I said, my voice filled with emotion. "These young people have shown me that change is possible. Together, we are rewriting our narratives."

Reflections on My Journey

As I stood there, I reflected on the journey that had brought me to this moment. I thought about the darkness I had faced, the choices that led me to prison, and the resilience I had discovered within myself. Each experience has shaped me, preparing me for this mission of helping others.

The path of purpose is not always clear, but I knew I was on the right track. I had built a community, forged connections, and embraced my role as a mentor. With every workshop, and every story shared, I felt more aligned with my purpose.

Looking Ahead

As I look to the future, I am filled with excitement and determination. There are still challenges ahead, but I am ready to face them. I will continue to advocate for change, inspire others, and seek growth opportunities.

This journey is far from over; it's just the beginning. I am committed to walking this path of purpose, not only for myself but for those who have yet to find their way.

With each step forward, I carry the lessons of my past, knowing that my story can inspire others to rewrite their narratives. Together, we can create a brighter future—a future filled with hope, resilience, and possibility.

Chapter 9

A New Chapter

I sat on the porch of my small apartment, the sun setting in the distance, painting the sky in hues of orange and pink. It felt like a perfect metaphor for my life—a blend of trials and triumphs, slowly shifting towards something beautiful. Reflecting on the journey that had brought me here, I couldn't help but feel a sense of gratitude for the path I had chosen.

Rebuilding Relationships

After my release, one of my top priorities was to rebuild the relationships I had fractured during my time in prison. My family, who had stood by me through thick and thin, deserved more than just my apologies; they deserved my commitment to change.

I arranged a family dinner, the first of many attempts to reconnect. My mother, her hands trembling with excitement, prepared my favorite dishes—collard greens, cornbread, and fried chicken. As we gathered around the table, the familiar scents filled the room with warmth and nostalgia.

"Jamal, I'm so proud of you," she said, tears glistening in her eyes. "You've come a long way."

Her words ignited a fire within me. "I'm determined to make you proud every day, Mom," I promised, my voice steady. This was my chance to show her that the boy she once lost was now a man with a purpose.

Forging New Connections

Rebuilding my life also meant forming new connections. I immersed myself in the community, volunteering at local organizations and attending support groups. I wanted to be surrounded by people who understood my journey, and who could lift me during moments of doubt.

One evening, while volunteering at a community center, I met Rachel, a passionate advocate for at-risk youth. Her enthusiasm was infectious, and we quickly bonded over our shared mission. She introduced me to her network of mentors, counselors, and activists, all dedicated to uplifting those in need.

"Jamal, your story could inspire so many," Rachel said one day, her eyes shining with excitement. "You should consider speaking at our next community event."

At first, I hesitated. The thought of speaking publicly filled me with anxiety. But deep down, I knew it was an opportunity to make a difference. I agreed, ready to share my journey and inspire others to overcome their challenges.

A Night to Remember

The night of the event arrived, and I found myself backstage, pacing. The auditorium was filled with faces eager to hear stories of hope. As I listened to the speakers before me, I reminded myself why I was there.

When my name was called, I stepped onto the stage, the spotlight warming my skin. My heart raced, but I took a deep breath, focusing on the message I wanted to share.

"Good evening, everyone," I began, my voice shaking slightly. "My name is Jamal, and I stand before you as a testament to the power of change. I was once lost in a cycle of despair, but I chose to rewrite my story."

As I spoke, I saw heads nodding in understanding, and I felt a connection to the audience. I shared the struggles I faced in prison, the hope that came from unexpected places, and the determination that propelled me forward.

By the time I finished, the room erupted in applause. I stepped off the stage, feeling lighter, as if I had shed the weight of my past. It was a pivotal moment—a realization that my journey could empower others.

Continuing My Education

With newfound confidence, I decided to further my education. I enrolled in community college, aiming to earn a degree in social work. It was a decision rooted in my desire to understand the systemic issues that led many like me down a dark path.

The classes were challenging, but I was committed. I connected with professors who inspired me and classmates who shared my passion for social change. Every assignment and lecture fueled my desire to create a meaningful impact in the community.

One day, I wrote a paper about rehabilitation programs and their effectiveness in reducing recidivism. It resonated with my experiences, and I knew this was an area I wanted to explore further. My professor encouraged me to present my findings at an upcoming conference, and though nervous, I accepted the challenge.

A Leap of Faith

Presenting at the conference was an exhilarating experience. I spoke to a diverse audience of educators, policymakers, and fellow advocates. Sharing my insights felt like a culmination of my journey—a chance to advocate for change on a larger scale.

After my presentation, attendees approached me with words of encouragement. "Your story is powerful," one woman said. "We need more voices like yours in this conversation."

At that moment, I realized that my experiences weren't just personal; they were part of a larger narrative that needed to be told. I was committed to being a voice for those still trapped in the cycle of incarceration and poverty.

Giving Back to the Community

As I continued my studies, I sought ways to give back. I organized community workshops focused on life skills, resume building, and financial literacy for young adults. It was vital for me to provide tools that could help others avoid the pitfalls I once faced.

During one workshop, a young woman named Lisa approached me. "I feel stuck like there's no way out," she admitted, her eyes downcast.

I listened intently as she shared her struggles, and I couldn't help but see my past reflected in her words. "Lisa, I know how you feel," I said gently. "But I'm living proof that change is possible. You have the power to rewrite your story, too."

Her eyes widened with hope, and I felt a sense of purpose surge within me. I knew I was making a difference, one person at a time.

Creating a Lasting Impact

As the months passed, I began to see the impact of my work. Participants from my workshops reached out to share their successes—getting jobs, enrolling in school, and pursuing their dreams. Their achievements fueled my passion to keep going.

I decided to launch a mentorship program through the nonprofit to pair young adults with experienced mentors who could guide them in their journeys. I wanted to create a ripple effect, inspiring others to lift each other and build a supportive community.

The program took off, and I found joy in watching mentees thrive. Their growth was a testament to the power of connection, understanding, and support.

Looking Toward the Future

As I sat on the porch that evening, I felt a profound sense of peace. My journey has been filled with ups and downs, but every experience has shaped me into who I am today. I was determined to keep moving forward and to continue making an impact in the lives of others.

The journey ahead was uncertain, but I embraced it with open arms. I envisioned a future where I could advocate for change, support those in need, and foster a sense of community.

This was my new chapter—a life dedicated to purpose, resilience, and hope. I had come a long way from the darkness that once consumed me, and I was ready to face whatever lay ahead.

A Call to Action

As I closed my eyes, I whispered a silent prayer of gratitude. I thought about the young men and women still caught in the cycle of despair. I promised myself to keep advocating for them and to use my voice to inspire change.

"Your story matters," I reminded myself. "It has the power to ignite hope in others."

With that thought, I stepped into the future, ready to write the next chapter of my life—a chapter filled with purpose, passion, and the unwavering belief that change is possible.

Chapter 10

Guide to Life After Prison: Practical Steps for Reintegration and Success

Reintegrating into society after time behind bars is a journey filled with challenges, triumphs, and setbacks. However, with the right mindset and tools, you can create a successful life for yourself. In this chapter, we'll walk through several essential areas that will support your reentry into the world. From rebuilding relationships to finding work, managing finances, and maintaining your mental health, this guide offers real, practical steps to help you on the path to success.

1. Building a Support Network

One of the most important aspects of life after prison is having a strong support network. No matter how determined you are, the journey will be easier if you are surrounded by people who care for you, believe in you, and can offer encouragement when you face challenges.

A. Leaning on Family and Friends

For many people, family is the foundation of support after release. However, relationships with family members may have been strained or broken due to past behaviors or simply the time spent apart. Rebuilding these relationships will require patience and humility.

- **Rebuilding Trust**: Trust is something that may have been lost during your time away, but it can be regained. Start by being honest with your loved ones. Acknowledge the mistakes you've made, but also share your vision for a better future. Make promises only if you know you can keep them, and be consistent in your actions. Trust is earned through repeated actions over time.

- **Offering Apologies and Understanding**: Your family may have been hurt by your past choices, and part of rebuilding relationships means addressing that pain. Offer sincere apologies where necessary, but also give your loved ones the space to process their feelings.

- **Setting Healthy Boundaries**: While family is important, it's also crucial to set healthy boundaries, especially if some family members are negative influences. Surround yourself with people who support your growth, even if it means limiting contact with those who might drag you down.

B. Finding New Support Systems

- **Mentorship Programs**: Many organizations offer mentoring programs for formerly incarcerated individuals. These programs pair you with someone who has walked the same path and understands the specific struggles of reentry. A mentor can offer guidance, encouragement, and practical advice on how to navigate life after release.

- **Support Groups**: Faith-based groups, community organizations, and nonprofits often run support groups for returning citizens.

These groups provide a safe space where you can share your experiences, learn from others, and receive emotional support during difficult times.

C. Letting Go of Toxic Relationships

It's hard to succeed if the people around you are pulling you back into old habits. Letting go of toxic friendships and relationships is one of the hardest but most necessary steps for your growth. If you have friends or family members who are involved in criminal activities, drug abuse, or negative influences, you need to distance yourself from them.

2. Overcoming Stigma and Rejection

Society often places labels on those who have been incarcerated, and overcoming this stigma is one of the most challenging aspects of reentry. You may face rejection when applying for jobs, housing, or even social circles. However, remember that rejection is not the end of the road—it's a detour that can lead you to new opportunities.

A. Changing the Narrative

One of the first steps in overcoming societal stigma is to change how you see yourself. You are not defined by your past mistakes; you are defined by how you respond to them. When others try to label you, respond with confidence in your transformation. Practice explaining your story in a way that shows your growth and the lessons you've learned.

- **Elevator Pitch**: Practice a brief, positive way of explaining your background that focuses on your future. For example, "Yes, I made mistakes in the past, but those mistakes helped me grow. Now I'm focused on using what I've learned to make better choices and help others."

B. Dealing with Rejection

Rejection is hard, but it's part of life after prison. When a potential employer or landlord turns you down, it can feel personal, but it's essential to keep moving forward.

- **Persistence Pays Off**: Don't let one "no" stop you. Keep applying for jobs and housing, and eventually, the right opportunity will come. Every rejection is one step closer to the "yes" you're waiting for.

- **Use Resources**: Several organizations are designed to help formerly incarcerated individuals find jobs, housing, and other services. Use these resources to increase your chances of success.

3. Finding Employment After Prison

One of the biggest challenges after prison is finding a stable job. Employers may be hesitant to hire someone with a criminal record, but there are steps you can take to increase your chances of success.

A. Honesty in Applications

It's important to be honest about your past when applying for jobs. Many employers conduct background checks, and being caught in a lie can cost you an opportunity. Instead of hiding your record, focus on how you've changed and what you've learned from your experiences.

- **Addressing Your Record in Interviews**: If asked about your criminal record in an interview, be upfront but steer the conversation toward your rehabilitation and the positive steps you've taken since your release. Explain what you've learned and how you plan to use that knowledge to contribute to their organization.

B. Building Skills

The job market is competitive, and having valuable skills can set you apart from other candidates. If possible, use your time in prison to build skills that are in demand.

- **Education Programs**: Many prisons offer educational programs where you can earn a degree or certification. Even after your release, you can continue learning through community colleges, vocational schools, or online courses.

- **Apprenticeships and Trade Jobs**: Some industries, like construction, trucking, or culinary arts, are more open to hiring formerly incarcerated individuals. Consider learning a trade skill that can lead to stable employment.

C. Employers That Hire Ex-Offenders

Several companies are open to hiring people with criminal records. Research these companies and apply to those that have a history of giving second chances. In addition, nonprofits and community organizations often have job placement programs specifically for returning citizens.

4. Staying Mentally and Emotionally Healthy

The mental and emotional strain of reentry is often overlooked, but it is a critical part of your success. Prison life can take a toll on your mental health, and the challenges of reintegration can exacerbate this stress.

A. Dealing with the Psychological Effects of Incarceration

Many people leave prison with anxiety, depression, or PTSD due to the trauma of incarceration. It's important to acknowledge these feelings and seek help if necessary.

- **Therapy and Counseling**: Seeking professional help is not a sign of weakness—it's a smart way to take control of your mental health. Many counselors specialize in working with formerly incarcerated individuals, and they can offer coping strategies for dealing with stress, trauma, and anxiety.

- **Self-Care Practices**: Simple self-care practices like regular exercise, meditation, journaling, or engaging in a hobby can help you manage stress and maintain emotional balance.

B. Avoiding Triggers and Negative Influences

Life after prison is full of temptations to fall back into old patterns. Staying mentally healthy involves recognizing these triggers and finding ways to avoid them.

- **Identifying Triggers**: Be aware of the people, places, and situations that trigger negative emotions or behaviors. Whether it's seeing an old friend who was a bad influence or visiting neighborhoods that remind you of past mistakes, knowing your triggers can help you avoid them.

- **Replacing Negative Habits with Positive Ones**: Instead of going back to old habits, focus on building new, positive routines. Whether it's exercising, reading, volunteering, or working, filling your time with productive activities can keep you on the right path.

5. Avoiding Old Traps and Temptations

The pull of old habits and environments can be strong, especially in the early stages of reentry. It's essential to stay vigilant and avoid the traps that led you into trouble in the first place.

A. The Company You Keep

Your environment plays a significant role in your success. Surround yourself with people who support your growth and distance yourself from those who drag you back into destructive behaviors.

- **Choosing Positive Influences**: Look for people who are also trying to better their lives. Whether through support groups, faith communities, or mentors, being around people with positive attitudes can help you stay focused on your goals.

- **Recognizing Warning Signs**: Sometimes, you'll be tempted to slip back into old ways. Recognizing the warning signs—such as being around people who glorify crime or drugs—can help you avoid falling back into those traps.

B. The Importance of Saying "No"

Learning to say "no" to situations that threaten your progress is a skill you need to develop. Whether it's declining a party invitation or distancing yourself from old friends, saying "no" is a sign of strength, not weakness.

6. Financial Literacy for a Fresh Start

Managing your finances effectively is critical for building stability after prison. Without financial knowledge, it's easy to fall into debt, overspending, or even relapse into illegal activities.

A. Budgeting and Saving

Learning how to manage your money starts with creating a budget. A budget helps you understand how much money you have, how much you can spend, and how much you need to save.

- **Tracking Your Income and Expenses**: Keep a record of how much you earn and where you spend it. This can help you identify areas where you can cut costs and save for future goals.

- **Building an Emergency Fund**: Even if you can only save a small amount, putting money aside for emergencies can help you avoid financial crises in the future.

B. Building Credit

Having a good credit score can open doors for you, such as being able to rent an apartment or get a loan. Start building your credit by paying bills on time and, if possible, getting a secured credit card.

C. Avoiding Financial Traps

Be wary of financial traps such as payday loans or high-interest credit cards, which can lead to debt. Always read the fine print before signing any financial agreements.

7. Continuing the Journey of Self-Improvement

Reentry is just the beginning of your journey. To continue growing, you need to focus on ongoing self-improvement.

A. Education and Personal Development

Education doesn't have to stop after you leave prison. Whether through formal schooling, self-study, or community classes, continuing your education can help you build a better future.

- **Finding Opportunities for Growth**: Look for local programs that offer GED classes, vocational training, or even college courses. Many community centers and nonprofits offer free or low-cost education for returning citizens.

- **Lifelong Learning**: Beyond formal education, commit to lifelong learning. Read books, listen to podcasts, attend workshops, or take up a new hobby. Learning new things keeps your mind sharp and opens up new opportunities.

B. Giving Back to Others

One of the most rewarding aspects of personal growth is helping others. Whether it's volunteering at a community center, mentoring at-risk youth, or simply sharing your story with those still incarcerated, giving back can provide a sense of purpose and fulfillment.

- **Mentoring the Next Generation**: Use your experiences to guide others who are at risk of following the same path. Many organizations offer mentorship programs where you can help youth or recently released individuals navigate the challenges of life after prison.

- **Creating Lasting Change**: Whether it's through advocacy, volunteering, or community work, you have the power to create lasting change in your community. Your story can inspire others to turn their lives around and make a difference.

Conclusion: The Journey Continues

Life after prison is filled with challenges, but it's also filled with opportunities for growth and transformation. By building a strong support network, finding meaningful work, managing your finances, and staying mentally healthy, you can create a successful and fulfilling life. Your past does not define you—your actions today and tomorrow do.

Epilogue

Letters to My Younger Self

Dear Jamal,

If you're reading this, it means you've finally found a moment of quiet amidst the chaos of your life. I wish I could reach back through time and speak directly to you, to the boy filled with anger, fear, and confusion, standing at the crossroads of your life.

To the Boy in the Mirror

I see you—standing in front of the mirror, eyes filled with defiance and sorrow. You wear your pain-like armor, believing it makes you strong, but it only shields you from the light. The streets have taught you survival, but they've also taught you to numb your heart. You think you're alone in this fight, but trust me when I say you're not. There is so much more to you than the mistakes you're making.

Choices Matter

The choices you're making now will shape your future. I know you feel trapped like there's no way out, but every decision you make is a step on a path. You're heading down a road that will only lead to despair, and I urge you to pause and reflect.

You don't have to follow the same path as everyone around you. Seek out the people who want to lift you, not pull you down.

Hope is a Choice

I want you to understand something vital: hope is not a weakness; it's your greatest strength. It's the flicker of light in the darkest of places. Embrace it. Surround yourself with those who inspire you to be better, those who believe in your potential even when you can't see it. Remember, every moment of kindness you extend to others will come back to you tenfold.

It's Okay to Ask for Help

Don't be afraid to ask for help. The world doesn't expect you to carry your burdens alone. The real strength lies in vulnerability—allow yourself to be seen, to be heard. Find mentors, teachers, and friends who will guide you toward a brighter future. You'll be surprised at how many people want to help if you just let them in.

Redemption is Possible

Prison may feel like the end of the world, but it's just the beginning of a new chapter. The walls may close in around you, but within those confines lies an opportunity for growth. Embrace the struggle; it will mold you into the person you were meant to be. The pain you feel now is not the end; it's the catalyst for your transformation.

Forgiveness is Freedom

As you move forward, learn to forgive—not just others but yourself. You've made mistakes, yes, but they don't define you. Let go of the guilt and shame that weigh you down. Understand that forgiveness is not just for those who hurt you; it's a gift you give yourself. It's the key that will unlock your heart and set you free.

The Future is Yours to Create

You may not see it now, but the future is filled with endless possibilities. Your experiences will make you a beacon of hope for others who walk the same path. Use your story to uplift those still lost in darkness. Help them find their way back to the light.

Embrace Your Purpose

You're on the brink of discovering your purpose. Every setback is a setup for a comeback. The journey you're on may be long and arduous, but each step forward counts. Trust in the process and keep moving forward. Embrace the man you are becoming, and never forget the lessons you've learned along the way.

A Letter for the Future

So, if you ever doubt yourself, read this letter again. Let it be a reminder that change is possible and that you have the strength to rewrite your story.

When you stand on that stage one day, sharing your journey with others, remember that every struggle is worth it. You are proof that hope, resilience, and love can conquer even the darkest of circumstances.

Keep going, Jamal. The world is waiting for you.

With all my heart,
Your Future Self

This final message serves as both a personal reflection and a call to anyone who has faced their battles. May it inspire hope and the belief that no matter where you start, it's possible to find a path to purpose and redemption.

Printed in Great Britain
by Amazon